IMAGES
of America

WINONA LAKE

The train depot at Spring Fountain Park was across the street from the hotel and had a welcoming view of what was then called Eagle Lake, later known as Winona Lake. The original plot of 127 acres was deeded by Pres. Martin Van Buren in 1837. On May 6, 1881, the Beyer brothers, who were entrepreneurs, purchased 94 of those acres, later acquiring more. They began as produce men and sold butter and eggs. They were attracted to the cooling springs and the beautiful setting, initially because the springs could keep their products cool and fresh for a longer time. The many springs and the picturesque setting on Eagle Lake inspired them to call it Spring Fountain Park. The Beyers were instrumental in turning the area into a well-known attraction.

On the Cover: The bathing pavilion on Winona Lake attracted sun worshippers and water lovers. The electrified "Venetian Night" on the canal was visible from this area as boats were turned into beautiful floats and paraded in front of grandstands erected nearby. The pavilion and Winona Lake were at the height of glory in 1911, when thousands came each summer to enjoy all that was offered to vacationers and those looking for family activities.

Al Disbro

ISBN 9781531663940

Published by Arcadia Publishing
Charleston, South Carolina

Library of Congress Control Number: 2012939012

For all general information, please contact Arcadia Publishing:
Telephone 843-853-2070
Fax 843-853-0044
E-mail sales@arcadiapublishing.com
For customer service and orders:
Toll-Free 1-888-313-2665

Visit us on the Internet at www.arcadiapublishing.com

Dedicated to Jo, whose inspiration and creativity started the project.

Contents

ACKNOWLEDGMENTS

Thanks to Darla McCammon, a gifted writer and artist, who edited, organized, and reworked the sentences, making the stories more interesting. Thanks also to Luther Allen, Church of the Good Shepherd, Bill Darr, Steve Grill, Grace Schools, Kosciusko County Historical Society, Reneker Museum, Linda and Rex Snyder, Dr. Jane Heaton, John Heaton, Jerry Laurien, N. Bruce Howe Jr., Art Davis and Max Hay in memoriam, and the Van Dyke Family.

INTRODUCTION

A lake in the shape of a flying eagle is etched into the lands of northern Indiana, where the Potawatomi Indians once dwelled in the early 1800s. Appropriately, the tribe referred to that body of water as Eagle Lake. The name was later changed to Winona because of Sol Dickey and his former connection with the town Winona near Bass Lake in Starke County.

Winona Lake in Kosciusko County is located on the St. Lawrence continental divide, sending some waters north to the great lakes and others south through the Tippecanoe, Wabash, Ohio, and Mississippi Rivers. On the map, Winona Lake can be found about halfway between two of Indiana's largest cities: South Bend, the home of Notre Dame; and Fort Wayne, at the confluence of three rivers. Winona Lake is convenient to both cities and is only a two-hour drive from Chicago, which has helped it grow.

Since Potawatomi times, names have changed. The lake, originally referred to as Eagle Lake, was next called Spring Fountain Park by the Beyer brothers, who had the first major impact on the area; it later became Winona Lake and spawned the town of Winona Lake. From those beginnings, Winona Lake metamorphosed like a butterfly. By 1960, its wings spread from a tiny town of 2,000 to such fame that as many as 250,000 visitors competed to spend time there each season. Celebrities such as Will Rogers, Billy Graham, and novelist Theodore Dreiser flocked to Winona Lake. The town has spawned publishing companies; housed the national headquarters for religious groups; become the permanent residence of Billy Sunday, the former baseball player and charismatic preacher; been influential in the ministry of evangelist Billy Graham; and produced famous songs too numerous to list.

Notables, such as the owner of the Studebaker automobile factory in nearby South Bend, took an interest in Winona. Alexander McDonald, the president of Standard Oil, became involved and supported projects to benefit the community. World-famous religious leader D.L. Moody became a mentor to many in the little town on the periphery of Winona Lake. The board of directors of the Christian Assembly that formed in Winona Lake reads like a who's-who in the financial and political realm and, in addition to those mentioned above, included H.J. Heinz of Heinz ketchup, William Jennings Bryan, and William Carmichael.

Homer Rodeheaver, Billy Sunday, and Billy Graham created waves from Winona Lake that rippled throughout the world. The story of these men and their magnetism in music and preaching is an incredible testimony to the efforts they made in changing the lives of hundreds of thousands of people. Winona Lake, the backdrop for Rodeheaver's Rainbow Cottage and home of Billy and Ma Sunday, left a lasting impact whose tide may still be rippling ashore in some distant spot.

The rise, fall, and rebirth of Winona Lake is a story of trust, faith, perseverance, and—many would say—the hand of God.

Once again a bustling village, Winona Lake will steal the heart.

The Eagle Lake Hotel, built by the enterprising Beyer brothers, faced the train depot and also had a commanding view of the lake.

One

Before Winona
1890–1904

Spring Fountain Park, originally a plot of 127 acres on the banks of Eagle Lake, was deeded by Pres. Martin Van Buren to William Bashford on June 30, 1837. Upon Bashford's death in 1874, his family sold the property to Dr. Jacob Boss, whose son, Julius Boss, inherited it from his father. On May 6, 1881, the Beyer brothers bought 94 of those acres, adding more to the property later.

The Beyer brothers were entrepreneurs in many ways. They began as produce men and sold butter and eggs. They were initially attracted to the cooling springs and beautiful setting, because the springs could keep their products cool and fresh longer. The many springs and the picturesque setting on Eagle Lake inspired them to call it Spring Fountain Park.

In the 1890s, the prospering brothers developed the area as a summer resort, building a hotel and then a track for horses and bicycles on the land that would later become an island. Near the lake, they built an amusement ride called a "switch back" that operated a bit like a roller coaster and utilized gravitational pull to give riders a thrill. They created a toboggan slide and built fishponds and fountains. Lastly, they added a cyclorama to their entertainment resort.

Sailboats were a common scene on Winona Lake. In the background is the popular cyclorama, a large round building not unlike a fat farm silo, though not as tall. The cyclorama was introduced to the area by the Beyer brothers based on an invention by Irishman Robert Barker in Edinburgh in 1787. The cyclorama, a predecessor of the Cinerama and IMAX, was simply a panoramic painting done around the wall inside a cylindrical building. The first cyclorama for Winona Lake was on the lakefront and was an oil painting of the battles of the civil war at Chattanooga, Mission Ridge, and Lookout Mountain. Artist Harry Kellogg took five years to complete the painting. After a while, the subject was deemed not appropriate for the Christian family atmosphere and it was repainted with scenes from the life of Christ. Some cycloramas still exist today, notably in Atlanta and Gettysburg, but the Winona Lake Cyclorama is now a memory.

The Beyer Springs cooled produce and became a great attraction around the resort, especially when men of the day found they could catch a tasty cup of water out of a local tree.

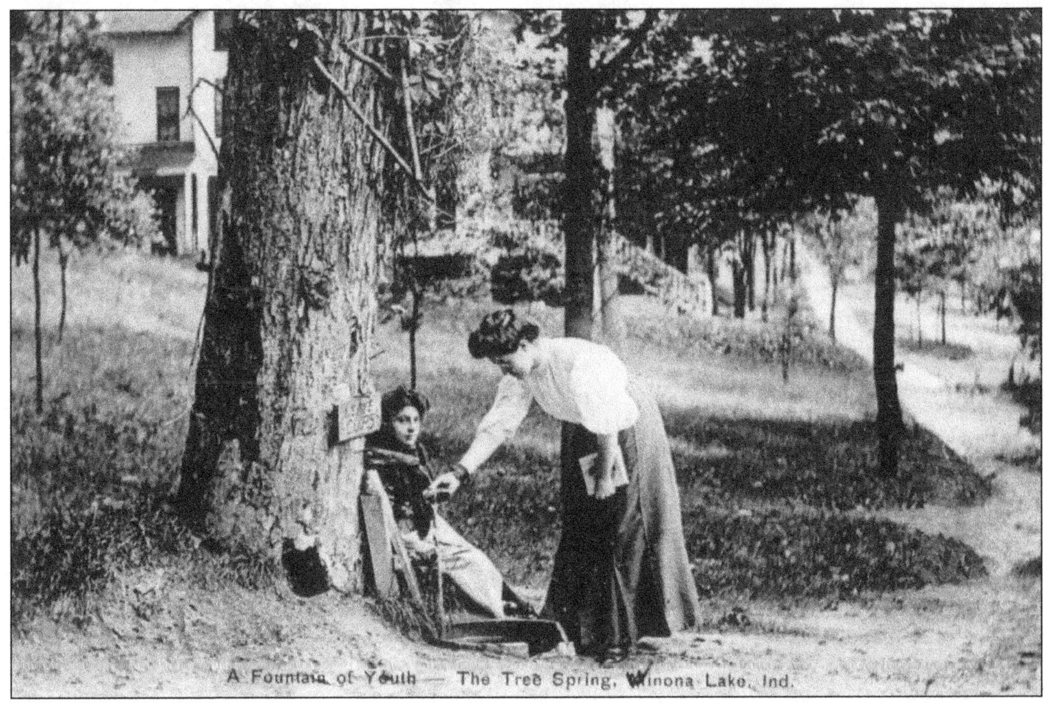

A Fountain of Youth — The Tree Spring, Winona Lake, Ind.

The Beyer Spring Fountain Park trees attracted women as well. In those days, it was quite common to use a "community" tin cup.

The Spring Fountain Park amusement center promoted a family atmosphere and catered to children such as these, who are getting a joy ride in a buggy pulled by a well-trained horse.

Sol Dickey, the superintendent of home missions of the Presbyterian church, had a dream. His dream resulted in this auditorium, which was set up for a missionary convention. Dickey liked Chautauqua Lake in New York, where the popular Chautauqua summer educational camps for adults began. Dickey was prompted to create a summer Chautauqua but struggled to find a location. He found Bass Lake in Starke County, Indiana, and a small community called Winona. The county commissioners gave him an option on 200 acres and promised to build a branch of the C&E railroad to the lake. The Winona Assembly was thus formed as a corporation, but the commissioners did not fulfill their part of the bargain. The site was abandoned, as Dickey would not open a site without good public access.

Dickey, under pressure to have a place ready for his summer school of 1895, happened to meet one of the Beyer brothers traveling from Chicago. They struck up a conversation and Dickey shared his concerns about how his dreams for his Christian Chautauqua were not coming to fruition. Beyer saw this as an opportunity and told Dickey, "We are located just east of Warsaw on the banks of beautiful Eagle Lake. We already have a hotel and park located there. A railroad with a depot provides good access and is just across from our hotel where the train stops—oh, and by the way, we are interested in selling." The three Beyer brothers are seen here around the time they met Dickey.

Sol Dickey visited Spring Fountain Park and fell in love with the setting and the possibilities. The Beyer family was amenable to his ideas and soon struck a deal, selling the property to him and financing the proposition.

The first local summer Chautauquas were called Beyer summer programs, and later, by the time of this photograph, Winona Assembly programs. Soon, the names Winona Hotel, Winona Lake, and Winona Park began to be used. In 1904, bowing to popular usage, the Beyer brothers began using the same terminology, and in 1913, the town was incorporated as Winona Lake and Eagle Lake became Winona Lake. Had the funds been available to connect the C&E railroad to Dickey's original location, the park would have been known as Bass Lake at Winona in Starke County and what we now know as Winona Lake would be just another part of the city of Warsaw on the banks of Eagle Lake.

Popular almost immediately, Winona Park was an attractive place for a buggy ride. What was once known as a wilderness became a place for education, enrichment, and enjoyment through the efforts of several enterprising citizens.

A ticket window was necessary for entrance to the Winona Assembly grounds as word began to spread about the good experiences people were having there. As the reputation grew, many new people were drawn to the attractions each year.

This early view shows another angle of the old auditorium. Note the trees, many planted by the Beyer family, for which the area became noted. In fall, the foliage was ablaze, also drawing many admirers.

Before automobiles, attire and conveyances like this were the norm. This photograph is from the personal collection of Homer Rodeheaver, an important figure in the later development of the area.

The resort had several ponds, only one of which is still in existence. Most were built by the Beyer brothers. The grounds were landscaped and managed in order for visitors to be able to find tranquil areas in which to relax and reflect. This pond was called the Floral Pond.

The crowds continued to grow larger during this era. Notice the miniature rail tracks in the foreground. The small railroad carried luggage from the entrance to Kosciusko Lodge, one of several cottages available for visitors to the area.

In later times, as the automobile began making an appearance, changes had to be made to the entrance in order to accommodate the new mode of arrival. Prior to this, horse-drawn vehicles and trains were the primary form of transportation to Winona Lake.

In those days, the houses did not have numbers. Instead, they had colorful names, like the Muffet House seen here.

What later became Argonne Road at one time included a golf course, in the foreground of this photograph. To the left is the depot, with the hotel towering behind it overlooking the lake. The peninsula jutting across the top was a low-lying area with a racetrack and bicycle track that often became soggy. The racing tracks later became an elevated island, which was dredged out to form a new housing development along with a canal. The island played an important role in later developments. The main entrance to the resort was on the right.

Two men take a ride along the lake, their silk high-top hats gleaming in the sun. Winona Lake, at this time still only lightly populated, provided more undisturbed and scenic views than in later years.

The auditorium underwent facelifts such as new awnings and other upgrades. The crowds changed the way they dressed with each new season. Attendance continued to grow as word spread about the benefits of attending the assembly.

Staying with the tradition of giving names to homes, Sunrise was the second house built in Winona. It still stands at the corner of Fifth and Chestnut Streets. The first home erected in the city no longer exists but was also built on Chestnut Street. It was replaced by the Free Methodist Church parking lot.

The Winona Hotel on the left and the entrance on the right hold court over the lake and the railroad depot. Note the convenient access from the train tracks to the activities waiting at the two buildings.

The depot was renamed from Eagle Lake to Winona Lake after 1904. The availability of this depot was a turning point in the lake's history.

Golfing was another available activity for visitors to the area. Golf attire was much more formal in those days and most clubs had handmade wooden shafts. Here, two gentlemen prepare to tee off.

This old postcard features a drawing over a photograph with the hotel in the background. The drawing depicts a woman calling "fore" as she swings her driver off the tee. Many visitors took advantage of the links for a day of enjoyable golfing during their stay.

The "community cup" remains in evidence through the years and the tree "spring" water continues to be enjoyed by all as clothing styles evolve over time.

This reflecting pool, called the Trout Pond, was popular at the time and saw much activity, but over time, it may have naturally filled in and has since disappeared.

This scenic dirt road, Lake Shore Drive, ran in front of the hotel. Lodgers could take an enjoyable buggy ride along the edge of the tree-lined drive and view Winona Lake from many different angles. The sunsets were often spectacular and could be viewed from this direction, which ran along the eastern shoreline, and thus faced the setting sun. Today, this thoroughfare is called Park Avenue.

The Carp Pond was a favorite spot for the white domestic ducks imported to the pond for the enjoyment of guests. Note more of the landscaping efforts along the attractively trellised walkway in the background.

Many springs continued to flourish in Winona Lake long after the name was changed from Spring Fountain Park. This particular spring, providing a cooling sip for the lady with the bustle and the chic bonnet, was called Rock Spring.

More chic bonnets were in evidence when this crowd eagerly awaited their turn to enter the auditorium and participate in the Christian Chautauqua.

With no refrigeration other than the cooling springs, the Winona Lake Ice Company made a nice income carving ice out of Eagle Lake in the winter and keeping it for summer in the Beyer spring-cooled storage. Local children ran after the ice wagon and hoped for chips of ice on hot days.

An artist's rendition of people on the shore of Winona Lake was used on this postcard. Visitors sent the card, with a view of the swimmers, so friends and family could see the scenery.

"Hoosier" Hillside, taken from the nickname given to Indiana residents, was a row of homes, cottages, and lodging facilities available for visitors to rent during the assembly. While the term "Hoosier" refers to someone from Indiana, disagreements occur when Hoosiers are asked how the term came to be. Several theories abound but none have been verified as the correct answer.

A natural hillside overlooks Winona Lake. This row of homes on the hillside was called Fountain Row because it also faced some of the fountains below.

The Auditorium Promenade shows more evidence of the lavish landscaping of the day. Profuse arrangements of flowerbeds, gardens, and this pond made the walk to the auditorium enjoyable.

Boating was popular on the lake. The Beyer brothers provided a steamer for nautical trips to view the lake. This was one of their tickets.

A Spring Fountain Park bus coupon was good for seven trips on the Spring Fountain Park bus line. The purchaser of ticket No. 644 paid 50¢ for this coupon to ride the horse-drawn bus.

This early map shows Eagle Lake and the grounds and layout of the Spring Fountain Park racetrack area before it was dredged and made into an island with a canal. For two years, this area was a racetrack for horse racing and bicycling. The area was also utilized as an athletic field for other activities as needed. Betting was forbidden at the racetrack.

This map shows the bicycle course and athletic grounds prior to the dredging project. Note that it is labeled Winona as well as Eagle Lake in the title.

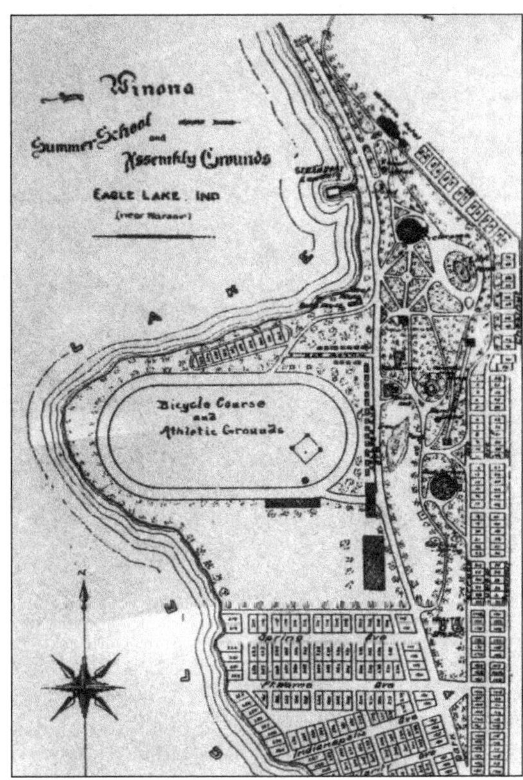

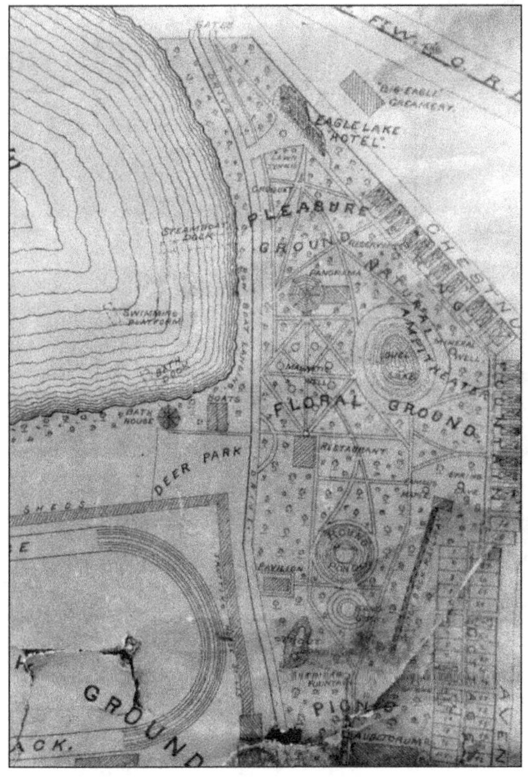

More detail of the elaborate grounds is seen in this 1890 map. Note the deer park near the racetrack.

The deer park had a population of white-tailed deer. The area also featured pony rides. The ponies were kept at the Beyer Farm and delivered to the park for children's rides on a daily basis. The Beyer Farm was located where Ace Hardware of Warsaw is now.

The army used the grounds for conducting drills and, during World War I, this area was used as a military base.

Two

THE BEGINNINGS 1904–1915

The Beyer brothers had a massive impact on Eagle Lake by developing it into a major amusement center and attraction called Spring Fountain Park. Some years after the inception of the park, and following their sale of the property to Sol Dickey for his Chautauquas, the town was incorporated as Winona Lake and the assembly began having its own impact on the area.

An advisor suggested digging a canal to create an island in place of the racetrack. This was accomplished and McDonald Island was born, with lots offered for sale. Sol Dickey obtained one such lot and built a home at one end of the island. Some existing structures from those early days of Spring Fountain Park, such as the cyclorama, continued to be used, while other structures, such as the boat house and the Westminster Hotel, were new additions.

Cottages and properties for rent were still available for visitors, but many new permanent homes were also built and, due to the lack of a street numbering system, were given such creative names as Merbrink, Toboggan, the Marshall Home, and Muffet House. Meanwhile, the roots of the Christian heritage so vital to the foundations of Winona Lake began to spread and became entrenched in the area. Unbeknownst to most of the local citizenry, they were witnessing events that would eventually send out emissaries from this area, electrifying the world and making this tiny place famous.

Transportation continued to evolve. Horses, buggies, bicycles, trains, automobiles, and airplanes all had an impact on the area. Local travel was affected by new changes as the area became increasingly popular.

Once the assembly became established, it was decided that it would be beneficial to sell lots for permanent residences. Benefactor Alexander McDonald, the vice president of Standard Oil of Kentucky, brought in a landscape architect who envisioned a large island. In order to create the island, he recommended dredging a canal on the easternmost side of the jutting land mass.

Once the dredging was begun on the canal, the lower areas of the old racetrack were filled in by spreading the soil pulled up from the bottom of the canal. The project raised the height of the island to a safe building level and McDonald Island was born. Homes were then built on the island using the technology of the time. Today, new homes are built on pilings for stability.

A young man enjoys a swing with a view from the hillside overlooking the new island and the lake. The hills on the east side of the lake have a beautiful vista and a mesa on the other side.

Many ponds existed on the property. The landscape designers created bridges and islands to increase the attractiveness of the gardens.

J. Wilbur Chapman figured in much of Winona history. His home was located on Center Street. It can still be seen today behind what was the old McDonald Hospital and current Papa John's near the famous Wagon Wheel Theater. Chapman was considered the father of the Winona Bible Conference.

Sol Dickey, the man with the farsightedness to purchase property from the Beyer Brothers, built a home with much character on the far end of the island facing the sunset. William Jennings Bryan, famous orator and politician, stayed in this home when visiting. The intriguing structure was called "Kilarney Castle." A short drive around the island will bring the castle into view. A man who worked for the Beyer brothers was quoted in the local *Times-Union* newspaper as having assisted with the construction of the Dickey home and said, "It was a custom of Dr. Dickey to keep a telescope in his study high in the tower. Since all visitors had to cross one of two bridges to the island, Dr. Dickey would know who was approaching his castle home. If the party was someone he wished to see, Dr. Dickey buzzed a signal to his wife downstairs."

The Mystery of Merbrink is also a love story. Ellen "Nellie" Cooper and her parents lived in Evansville, Indiana. Nellie and her parents moved to Winona Lake, after which her father died. Nellie and her mother began to manage a place called "The Inn" of 250 rooms where the Cerulean restaurant is now located. The pair eventually gained management of the Swiss Terrace because of Nellie's beau, William Brunning, who became wealthy from his import and export business dealings. He followed Nellie to Winona, purchased the Swiss Terrace, and in 1905 built the Merbrink home in hopes Nellie would marry him. It was a beautiful Victorian home, lavishly furnished. Brunning traveled weekly by rail to visit his love, but they did not marry until Nellie was 50 and her mother died. Once married, the Brunnings moved to Evansville but took vacations at Merbrink. Unfortunately, Nellie became ill and died. Brunning, a mysterious figure, left the home to his nephew. His will said, "My sister gets nothing, and she knows why." The Merbrink home eventually went up for sale by the sheriff. Don White purchased the home, which remains in his family as a summer home. Anna Lou, a daughter, recalls how the family had several encounters with a friendly ghost named Miss Phoebe who locals say resides in the home. Things were often misplaced, and these events were attributed to the ghost. Don White claimed to have seen her on the second floor when he was out on the lake fishing. The family told of many unexplained incidents during their days at Merbrink. Miss Phoebe was spotted once out on the second floor balcony by a local photographer who quickly snapped a picture, but the image came out showing all but the person.

Hillside cottage row held some of the available summer cottages lining a strip of land at the top of the hillside overlooking the lake. Here, two summer residents enjoy the lawn swing while a passerby stops to chat.

All homes in the town of Eagle Lake had names but no numbers. Some of the names were obvious and others were clever and creative. Homes such as Toboggan, Fountain View, Freifenheim, Idlewild, Sunrise, The Chicago, Sans Souci, and Merbrink were only a few of the interesting names. The family who owned Toboggan is seen here.

The cyclorama was a continuing attraction and drew crowds who wanted to experience the feeling of being wrapped in a three-dimensional work of art. The cyclorama was located between a pond and the lakefront. Parasols were common in those days for protection from the sun and the brilliant reflections coming off the water.

The shoreline and beach show paddleboats ready for enjoyment and the exciting amusement ride called the switchback, which operated with the pull of gravity, seen in the background.

The elaborate landscaping was one of the attractions that kept people returning year after year. The pond, the quaint bridges connecting the walks, and the flowering plants and shrubs were a continuous delight to visitors.

Walkers particularly enjoyed taking a stroll around the ponds and across the bridges, three of which are shown here. The grounds were immaculately landscaped, with new plantings of trees, shrubs, and flowering plants occurring on a regular basis.

The bathhouse was right next to the boathouse, where a restaurant exists today. Boaters could row or canoe along the canal and wind up at the boathouse and go, just beyond that, into the bathhouse to change out of their colorful swimwear and bathe.

The Westminster Hotel, with its canopied terrace entrance, was built in 1905 by the Presbyterian church—fondly called the "Presby" by old-timers. Later, in 1911, Homer Rodeheaver purchased Hall-Mack Publishers in Philadelphia and moved the business to the Westminster Hotel.

The Otterbein, with its "V" shaped entry in the corner, was a dormitory. Later, this structure was replaced by the Free Methodist church, which was built on the same foundation.

The entrance to the attractions evolved a great deal over the years. Blaine Mikesell and George Heaton each practiced their musical instruments upstairs in this building.

Another view shows the overall setting of the entrance. Notice the addition of another building and the train cars passing through. Only the serene lake in the background stayed consistent through the years.

The Marshall Home was named for the owner, who died before it was completed. Its intricate and ornamental structure was finished by his son, who donated its use for ministers and missionaries who might visit. The Remnant Trust was built in the same approximate location. The original building is long gone.

In comparison to the Marshall Home, the administration building shows the contrast and variety in architectural styles in Winona Lake. The administration building was the headquarters for the assembly. William Jennings Bryan held an office in this building when he was the secretary of state under Pres. Woodrow Wilson.

The beautiful Bedford limestone Beyer Home still stands today. This home and the brothers who built it became the wellspring for everything that began in this community. Two of the brothers lived in this home, with a family occupying each side and having their own private area. Both families shared a community living area and kitchen central to the home for entertaining and social gatherings.

This house on the corner of Park Avenue and Twelfth Street was originally called the Moody Building. It has since been the Evangel Hall, and finally, Bethany Hall.

This house is believed to have been owned by the Homer Rodeheaver family because photographs of the family were found in Rodeheaver's personal album with this home as their constant backdrop. The home towers over the area with a three-story view. Today, it is owned by Don Clemens.

The lovely, large Franconia, with its enduring Indiana limestone, commands a view many would covet. This home, owned by Bette Rodeheaver, has been a hotel, rooming house, and apartments. Notice the Baldwin just next door.

Before Billy Graham came on the scene in Winona Lake, another Billy, Billy Sunday, created quite a stir. Beginning as a professional baseball player who was called "the fastest man in baseball," Sunday's life was turned around when he heard a preacher at a revival in Pacific Gardens. Ultimately making Winona Lake his home base, he was known for some colorful quotes. Sunday once said, "When God turned the hose all out on Noah, the people were so foul a turkey buzzard couldn't fly over them without holding its nose." Sunday had a wife who was affectionately known as Ma Sunday. In 1915, she purchased land from the Winona Assembly for $576 and donated it to the Presbyterian Church. Sunday is shown here with the famous Glenn Curtis airplane that had been invited to Winona Lake for an exhibit. His sons are by his side.

A large crowd watched excitedly as aviator Glenn H. Curtiss demonstrated his hydro-aeroplane on Winona Lake. The event, on July 15, 1911, was one of the first such exhibitions on an inland lake. The combination boat and plane, later called a seaplane, landed and took off on the water in spite of a stiff breeze. Rev. Billy Sunday was treated to an afternoon ride, and chose to ride back with the pilot rather than walk back around the lake when the winds picked up and made it more dangerous to fly. Curtiss created a sensation that increased ticket sales and drew more than 15,000 people to enjoy the excitement. Sponsors of the event were amazed at the more than 1,000 automobiles at Winona Lake. The aviator, an early competitor of the Wright Brothers, staged his performance in front of Lake Side Stadium. Viewers were fortunate to see Curtiss, as he seldom flew at the time of the exhibition, keeping himself active in the business operation and with new inventions. Curtiss, in a rare admission that anything could possibly go wrong, said he kept his shoes untied in case he was forced to swim to shore.

The Winona Flyer was part of the Winona Interurban Railway train connection. Powered by electricity, the train traveled from Goshen to Peru with a stop at Winona Lake. Over the years, Winona Lake has incorporated many progressive forms of transportation.

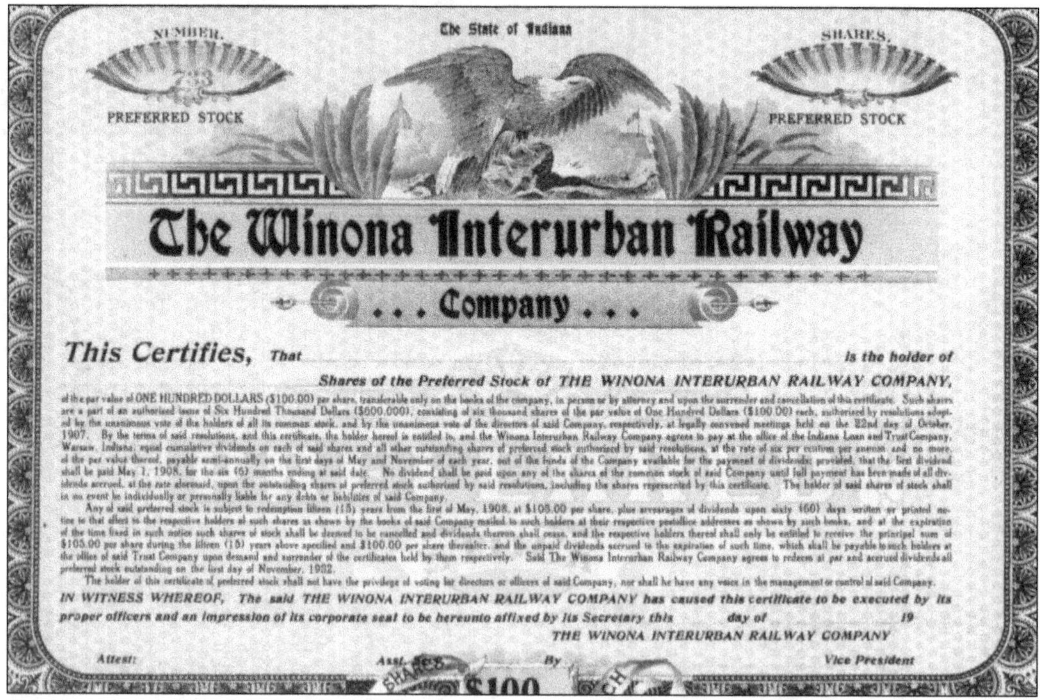

NUMBER. The State of Indiana SHARES.

PREFERRED STOCK PREFERRED STOCK

The Winona Interurban Railway

... Company ...

This Certifies, That ______ is the holder of ______ Shares of the Preferred Stock of THE WINONA INTERURBAN RAILWAY COMPANY, of the par value of ONE HUNDRED DOLLARS ($100.00) per share, transferable only on the books of the company, in person or by attorney and upon the surrender and cancellation of this certificate. Such shares are a part of an authorized issue of Six Hundred Thousand Dollars ($600,000), consisting of six thousand shares of the par value of One Hundred Dollars ($100.00) each, authorized by resolutions adopted by the unanimous vote of the holders of all its common stock, and by the unanimous vote of the directors of said Company, respectively, at legally convened meetings held on the 22nd day of October, 1907. By the terms of said resolutions, and this certificate, the holder hereof is entitled to, and the Winona Interurban Railway Company agrees to pay at the office of the Indiana Loan and Trust Company, Warsaw, Indiana, equal cumulative dividends on each of said shares and all other outstanding shares of preferred stock authorized by said resolutions, at the rate of six per centum per annum and no more, of the par value thereof, payable semi-annually on the first days of May and November of each year, out of the funds of the Company available for the payment of dividends; provided, that the first dividend shall be paid May 1, 1908, for the six (6) months ending at said date. No dividend shall be paid upon any of the shares of the common stock of said Company until full payment has been made of all dividends accrued, at the rate aforesaid, upon the outstanding shares of preferred stock authorized by said resolutions, including the shares represented by this certificate. The holder of said shares of stock shall in no event be individually or personally liable for any debts or liabilities of said Company.

Any of said preferred stock is subject to redemption fifteen (15) years from the first of May, 1908, at $105.00 per share, plus arrearages of dividends upon sixty (60) days written or printed notice to that effect to the respective holders of such shares as shown by the books of said Company mailed to such holders at their respective postoffice addresses as shown by such books, and at the expiration of the time fixed in such notice such shares of stock shall be deemed to be cancelled and dividends thereon shall cease, and the respective holders thereof shall only be entitled to receive the principal sum of $105.00 per share during the fifteen (15) years above specified and $100.00 per share thereafter, and the unpaid dividends accrued to the expiration of such time, which shall be payable to such holders at the office of said Trust Company upon demand and surrender of the certificates held by them respectively. Said The Winona Interurban Railway Company agrees to redeem at par and accrued dividends all preferred stock outstanding on the first day of November, 1932.

The holder of this certificate of preferred stock shall not have the privilege of voting for directors or officers of said Company, nor shall he have any voice in the management or control of said Company.

IN WITNESS WHEREOF, The said THE WINONA INTERURBAN RAILWAY COMPANY has caused this certificate to be executed by its proper officers and an impression of its corporate seal to be hereunto affixed by its Secretary this ______ day of ______ 19

THE WINONA INTERURBAN RAILWAY COMPANY

Attest: ______ Asst. Sec. ______ By ______ Vice President

SHARES $100 EACH

Sol Dickey, ever the entrepreneur, went to important people in many different towns and spoke with them about investing in the Winona Interurban Railway. The stock sold for $100 per share in 1907. Dickey and his group of supporters themselves invested a great deal of money in this new form of transportation because they felt it would provide a type of ongoing or endowment funding, whose return on investment could support the ministry activities well into the future.

The interurban required electrical power and this power building provided it, along with heat for the Winona Hotel and a number of homes in the area.

The cyclorama was near the lake, between the hotel and the boathouse. At first, the cyclorama had a painting of the civil war adorning its walls. Later, the painting was changed to match the Christian underpinnings and atmosphere of the area by depicting the life of Christ on the walls.

This view shows folks going to see the cyclorama. The crowds increased with each season. This angle shows the proximity to the lake of the large cyclorama building.

This home on McDonald Island, called Homedale, has a first-rate view of the Cyclorama structure.

Sol Dickey had a landscape architect build an attractive flowerbed for display. The next spring, a different architect from Indianapolis built the garden bed even higher. Visitors soon noted the raised bed and somehow the idea that it was an Indian mound popped into the minds of many of them. They repeatedly asked if it was an old Indian grave, since this was once the territory of the Potawatomi. The questions persisted until Dickey and Thomas Kane, the assembly president, decided to have the beds redone to quell the rumors. The height of the flowerbeds was reduced and plantings were designed to spell out the word Winona. Rumors still surface, even today, about the "Old Indian Mound" that was supposedly on the premises.

More flowerbeds—that were not imaginary Indian graves—existed along many of the beautiful walkways and carriage trails throughout the property.

Many varieties of boating were enjoyed on Winona Lake. Accommodations were made for anchoring all kinds and sizes of watercraft. These gentlemen were enjoying rowing in front of the cyclorama building.

It was not quite Venice, but the canal offered its own distinctly picturesque ride along the edges of the island. The canal was used extensively, and in recent years, it has been renovated and updated.

City of Warsaw was the name given to the first boat that began offering another method of arrival at Winona Lake. A channel, which still partially exists today as boat ramp access to Winona Lake, was cut until it reached the Warsaw Pennsylvania train depot. Passengers could disembark from the train at that depot rather than transferring somewhere and then taking a train to the Winona Lake depot. They could then enjoy a pleasant water voyage in order to arrive at their accommodations in Winona Lake. The boat was a unique steamboat, a bit top-heavy, as proven when its identical sister ship tipped over and sank. During this boat's time at Winona Lake, however, it provided a safe and enjoyable ride.

Transportation availability is critical to any enterprise and it was one of the main reasons Winona Lake was Sol Dickey's choice when he moved his assembly to the area. Multiple forms of transportation were explored through the years. Seen here is a separate small rail system that moved passengers and luggage from the Winona Lake depot to their accommodations at the hotel, the rental cottages, and other summer seasonal accommodations that were available. Word continued to spread about the ease of accessibility to the attractions, and crowds continued to grow during this time.

Dr J. Wilbur Chapman was a Presbyterian evangelist who traveled around the world with gospel singer Charles Alexander. Dr. Chapman was credited with being a mentor to his disciple, the former baseball player Billy Sunday, who went on to become a far-reaching evangelist based out of Winona Lake. At one time, Dr. Chapman was the director and founder of the Winona Lake Bible Conference. He passed away on Christmas Day in 1918, not long after he was made the moderator of the Presbyterian General Assembly.

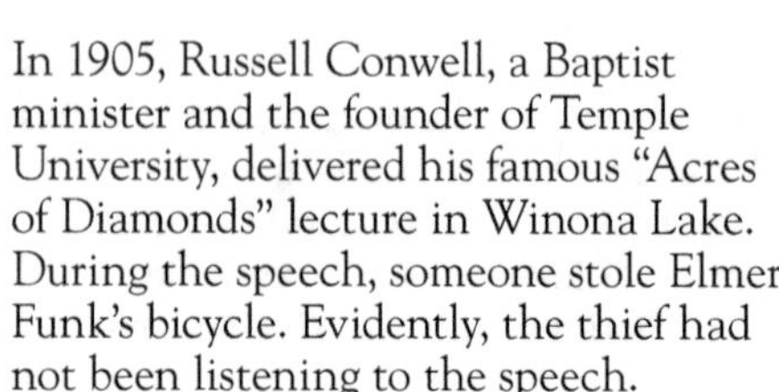

In 1905, Russell Conwell, a Baptist minister and the founder of Temple University, delivered his famous "Acres of Diamonds" lecture in Winona Lake. During the speech, someone stole Elmer Funk's bicycle. Evidently, the thief had not been listening to the speech.

The beginning events and founding activities were celebrated with an elaborate parade on July 4, 1911. Girls are wearing shorter skirts at this time, but female observers viewing the parade still have the longer gowns. By this time, bustles had gone out of style.

An equestrian portraying the Potawatomi and native heritages was an important part of the parade. Correct flag etiquette may not have been well known at this time, but patriotism was strong nevertheless.

The Winona Assembly for Boys stressed "Christian Character" on the sign they carried. Note the attire for the girls' tennis group compared to today. A great deal of work and effort went into the creation of the large arches, which drew much attention during the parade.

A rapt audience watched the large number of participants march through the arch. This photograph was taken from Park Avenue in front of the post office. The small building to the left was a drugstore at the time.

No parade is complete without music, and Winona Lake's proud musical heritage was evidenced with this lively band on Independence Day. The miniature train tracks that were used for transporting visitors and their luggage are visible on the far right as they wind their way into the distance.

Children, always a part of the family atmosphere of Winona Lake events, ride a beribboned float pulled by two prancing horses. Many activities were provided for children during the season while parents attended adult lectures and educational events. Note the distinct varieties visible at this time in the hats and head coverings the men are sporting. The gentleman on the left with the straw hat and baton directing things was Judson Van DeVenter, a friend of Wilbur Chapman and, later in life, a mentor to Billy Sunday. Van DeVenter, a graduate of Hillsdale College, was an instructor at the School of Photography and wrote the famous song "I Surrender All."

The entrance to Winona at one time had a large arch. For the parade, two large replicas were built to make it an impressive ceremony. These horses were decorated with feathered headgear and festooned with draping capes. They proudly pulled along a couple of beautiful young ladies and a young man in patriotic costume.

A variety of floats carried patriotic symbols and recreated historical events as they proudly came through the flag-adorned arches. Judson Van DeVenter (far left), a major source of inspiration to the parade committee, directs the floats and parade entries with his baton.

In the middle of this photograph, just behind the gentleman with the megaphone, is a Civil War veteran playing a big bass drum. The parade honored the veterans and celebrated the birth of the country. The large arches were a temporary construction.

Three

The Bible and the Artists 1915–1940

The Beyer brothers started it all. Sol Dickey stepped in and turned Winona Lake into something bigger that benefitted families. On June 2, 1913, the town of Winona Lake was incorporated officially with the name it was commonly called. Winona Lake continued to improve from the early 1900s through the advent of the automobile and the run-up to World War II.

This period saw famous artists, especially musical and dramatic actors or gifted orators, begin to appear and draw crowds at Winona Lake activities. New structures and gardens were built. The Chicago Boys Club came into existence when W. Clement Stone of Chicago delivered inner-city boys for a two-week summer camp. Games like roque, which was similar to croquet, drew large competitive crowds of admirers, Winona College was started in the Mount Memorial building, and a landmark structure called the Billy Sunday Tabernacle was built during this time.

Several of the buildings erected over these years are now remodeled foundational structures used by Grace School and College, which eventually supplanted Winona College. An improved fire department was needed after the great fire of 1914 devastated many structures. Reenactments of all kinds took place, celebrities of every type made their way here, and more tragedies came in the form of a heart-wrenching airplane crash, but the Winona Assembly and Bible Conference continued to have an impact that reached far beyond the perimeters of Winona Lake.

Winona Lake became a central point for much of what happened in Kosciusko County; all graduates from the various county schools held their commencement ceremonies at the lake. More famous landmarks were purchased, such as the statue that still exists in Winona Lake today, which was purchased by H.J. Heinz at the World's Fair in Paris. The "summer resort" atmosphere Winona Lake became famous for continued to attract permanent and seasonal residents. New schools of theology were formed in Winona Lake, too. People continued to seek quality family entertainment and enriching spiritual education to improve their lives, and Winona rewarded them.

Rowing along the canal in Winona Lake, boaters would eventually come to the boat house, where boats were stored under a roof. A restaurant now occupies the space.

This flag was reproduced from an original that was created after Winona Lake became a town on June 2, 1913.

Standing between the Swan Pond and the administration building are the Kosciusko County students who graduated that year. Commencement exercises were held at Winona Lake for a long time. Eventually, as the schools grew larger and the population expanded, the ceremonies were held at the individual schools.

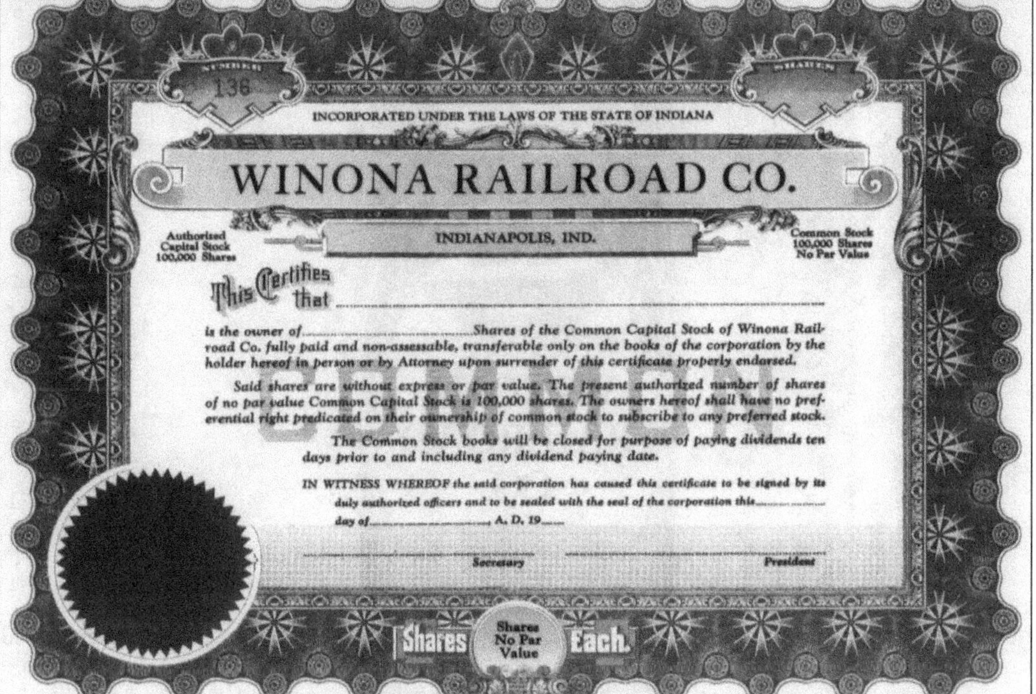

136

INCORPORATED UNDER THE LAWS OF THE STATE OF INDIANA

WINONA RAILROAD CO.

INDIANAPOLIS, IND.

Authorized Capital Stock 100,000 Shares

Common Stock 100,000 Shares No Par Value

This Certifies that ....

is the owner of .... Shares of the Common Capital Stock of Winona Railroad Co. fully paid and non-assessable, transferable only on the books of the corporation by the holder hereof in person or by Attorney upon surrender of this certificate properly endorsed.

Said shares are without express or par value. The present authorized number of shares of no par value Common Capital Stock is 100,000 shares. The owners hereof shall have no preferential right predicated on their ownership of common stock to subscribe to any preferred stock.

The Common Stock books will be closed for purpose of paying dividends ten days prior to and including any dividend paying date.

IN WITNESS WHEREOF *the said corporation has caused this certificate to be signed by its duly authorized officers and to be sealed with the seal of the corporation this............ day of............, A. D. 19....*

Secretary   *President*

COMMON

Shares — Shares No Par Value — Each.

Though much time had passed, Sol Dickey was still involved. He raised money for the Winona Railroad Company, selling stock for $100 per share.

This well-known sculpture, *The Student*, was purchased at the World's Fair in Paris in 1900. The sculpture adorned the grounds and is still part of Winona Lake today. H.J. Heinz, the ketchup baron and a wealthy board member of the assembly, also purchased statues of Venus and a lion of Canaan. Since some members believed the latter two were not appropriate for the park, they were not used.

Behind this limestone wall was a stone room built of variously sized local rocks. The underground room was kept cool by one of the natural springs prevalent in the area. The room was utilized for the storage of ice each year. Once the Beyer brothers no longer used the room, the founder of the Studebaker empire, out of South Bend, Indiana, had the spring plumbed into a fountain and built the wall. This popular place was named Studebaker Fountain.

G. Campbell Morgan (left) and Gypsy Smith (right) both came from London. Morgan was one of the founders of the Winona School of Theology. This photograph was taken just two houses north of the Beyer home. Morgan lived a few doors farther north.

The Winona School of Theology is seen here with its circular drive. The school was founded by G. Campbell Morgan, W.E. Biederwolf, and J.A. Huffman, who moved to Chicago shortly after the school was started.

The boathouse was a favorite gathering place. Rowboats were available to rent for excursions or for fishing trips on the lake, which was known for its good fishing conditions. Here, the passenger steamer *City of Warsaw* is in the canal at the side of the boathouse.

The Inn had over 230 rooms. Automobiles were beginning to make a difference in how many visitors obtained access to all the activities to be enjoyed at Winona Lake. This building was located close to and facing the water, but only a parking lot remains where the Inn once was.

For six weeks each year, Boys City, later changed to Chicago Boys Club, was in operation. The purpose of Boys City was to gather hundreds of wholesome boys from many cities into one large camp in the Winona woods. For three weeks, the goal was to teach them the meaning of good citizenship. The boys would have their own mayor and city officers and, interestingly, they were allowed to make their own laws. They also opened a bank and operated a grocery, a restaurant, a newspaper, a post office, and other enterprises.

Boys City was later purchased by W. Clement Stone, an influential, rags-to-riches entrepreneur from Chicago. He renamed it the Chicago Boys Club and encouraged inner-city young boys from Chicago to attend the summer camp. The goals were still the same and many young lives were positively affected by these camps. This area is now the Winona Greenway and a residential area called Stone Camp, named after W. Clement Stone.

With this glorious view of the bathhouse (left) and the boathouse in the background, it is easy to see how the water attracted hundreds of swimmers. A diving raft and piers provided ample opportunity to enjoy the fresh water of Winona Lake. Note the swimming attire including hats and caps.

These teams are playing a game called Roque, which is similar to croquet, except that the wickets are placed on a smooth, flat surface. Mallets and balls are used by the players in an attempt to make it around the maze of wickets with the fewest strokes. This game, yet another innovative and entertaining activity, helped keep visitors happy and occupied.

Kosciusko—pronounced Kah-SHOOS-ko by some and Kah-see-AHS-ko by others—Lodge was located south of Cherry Creek on Park Avenue, with a nice view of the lake. Note how places abound in the area for impromptu speeches and lectures, including these benches. Kosciusko County was named after a Polish Revolutionary War hero by the name of Kosciusko.

The Mount Memorial Building in Winona Lake once housed Winona College, which John Breckenridge founded in about 1905. There were two campus locations. The liberal arts school and the Technical and Agricultural Institute were located in Winona Lake. A separate Winona Technical Institute was in Indianapolis. Scientist Clarence Hickman was a notable graduate of Winona College.

The Mount Memorial Building is a commanding presence in the community. The building was named after Indiana governor James Mount. After Winona College moved out, the Grace Seminary program occupied the building, starting around 1939. Dr. Alva McLain and Dr. Homer Kent Sr. were responsible for bringing the seminary to the Mount Memorial Building and Winona Lake. During World War I, the army utilized the facility to train soldiers. Later, the building was the world headquarters of the Free Methodists. Today, Mount Memorial is beautifully renovated and houses administrative offices, classrooms, and the art department for Grace College of Winona Lake.

The Billy Sunday Tabernacle was a great landmark for the area. Tabernacles were built all over the United States as temporary structures for the Billy Sunday revivals. When lumberjacks went into the woods to cut timber for the buildings, a sawdust trail would be left behind so they could find their way out of the wilderness. Since the "lost" could be "found" with sawdust, a tradition came about to use sawdust on the floor at all Billy Sunday revival meetings. They called it "going down the sawdust trail." The tabernacle in Winona Lake was one of the last remaining structures of its kind in the United States. Eventually it had to be torn down, but through the generosity of Biomet founder Dane Miller, a small replica can be enjoyed today in the Remnant Trust Building. The Billy Sunday Tabernacle was also used for events other than religious services. On August 7, 1920, Madame Gali-Curci presented the first such concert to an enthusiastic audience. In 1921, former vice president Thomas R. Marshall spoke in the tabernacle. Other illustrious speakers such as Admiral Richard Byrd and James Whitcomb Riley were often the attraction. In 1925, audiences saw two concerts by John Phillip Sousa and the Marine Band. A world famous speaker filled the house in 1928 when Will Rogers was featured and brought the house down with his humorous anecdotes. George Heaton and Blaine Mikesell were in the audience and laughed with everyone when Rogers peeked around the corner of the curtain to see if the house was full. It was.

The Tabernacle was only used during clement weather because it offered no heat. In those days, the only air conditioning was the natural breeze off the lake. In spite of occasional discomfort in hot weather, the Tabernacle was almost always full.

The National Male Quartet included Jim Heaton (second from left), who shared how the quartet often sang a song written especially for them. The words were: "In trav'ling round, a fellow gets / in touch with lots of male quartets / but all admit there's very few / like Ray and Jim and Don and Lew."

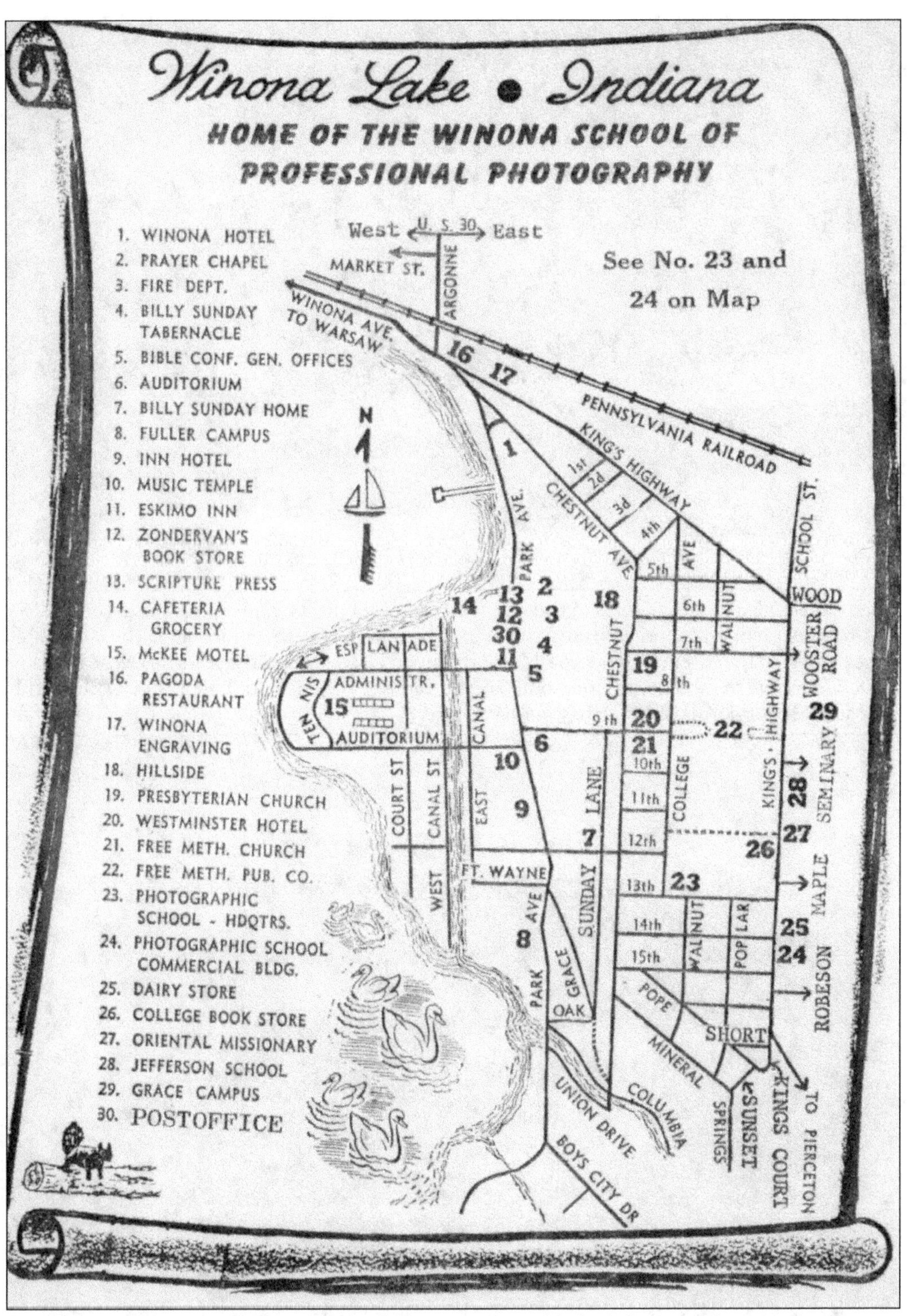

The Winona Lake School of Professional Photography published this map showing the locations of points of interest at the time. The interurban rail tracks were no longer in existence and only the Pennsylvania Railroad came through the area.

McKee Courts also gives evidence to the rise of the automobile. The interurban failed dismally as both an investment and a form of transportation. The founders were said to blame the automobile for the demise of the assembly; eventually, the financial losses caused the resort to close its doors. McKee Courts were motel-type units built in the center of the island. Later, they were used by Grace College for dorms. Today, they are backyards.

This closer view of the boat house shows where the rowboats were stored. A favorite activity for visitors was to rent a boat and row out through the canal and onto the lake.

In 1912, the students and staff of Winona College were treated to a boat ride on Winona Lake. Curious white ducks approached the boat in search of a possible meal.

In the early 1900s, an abundance of water may have caused an error in considering the safety of the community. As late as 1914, the only firefighting equipment in Winona Lake was a cart with a hand pump that connected to a hose on the bridge. The ineffectual spray of water it produced is seen here spraying into the canal during a practice session. Most of the homes in Winona Lake were built of flammable materials.

There was a brisk wind on April 18, 1914. Local residents raked leaves into a pile and set them on fire without considering wind direction. In moments, this error in judgment was revealed when a raging inferno quickly spread like a leaping gazelle across yards and buildings; soon, many homes and structures were engulfed in flames. Volunteers worked feverishly to extinguish the fire but a lack of equipment and trained manpower soon made it evident the wind and flames were winning the battle. M.F. Howe was working on the train tower at the time and contacted the city of Fort Wayne for help. Equipment was sent over immediately via train. A complete fire company with pumping machinery disembarked and pumped water from the lake.

Help arrived within an hour. Howe was forced to watch his own home burn. Two homes were dynamited in efforts to set up a backstop. They were able to save the hotel but, in the final count, 22 homes and summer cottages were destroyed by the fire, which followed a path along Chestnut Street to the hotel. Amazingly, there were only minor injuries and no casualties from this catastrophe.

Next to the smoldering ruins of a neighbor, this stone house on the corner of Fourth Street survived the conflagration. Onlookers gaze along the street that once held homes.

The Chicago, once a lovely home where friends gathered, was turned to ashes in the fire.

Building and living in an unpretentious home in Winona Lake, Billy Sunday traveled all over the world to reach others for Christ. Sunday and Homer Rodeheaver were the brains behind the creation of Easter sunrise services.

The Sunday family posed for this photograph. Sunday was a spirited, colorful character. One Sunday night, Jim Heaton and his son George were driving Billy Sunday to a service in Claypool, Indiana, just south of Winona Lake. A concerned Billy Sunday repeatedly told Heaton, "I should not have agreed to this service, there will only be a few people there." When they arrived, the place was already packed. Reverend Sunday hurriedly said to Heaton, "Get on in there and start leading the music." Heaton replied, "But Billy, the minister isn't here yet." Reverend Sunday, confident again, answered, "Go ahead, we don't need him!"

Plays and performances were always being produced in Winona Lake. Most of the actors were local. The traditions of music and drama and evangelism to the world continue in the community today.

Acting in productions with a moral purpose was considered an evangelistic calling by many. This tradition is still encouraged today, with high school productions of enriching music and drama throughout the community, and through the auspices of Grace College and programs such as Masterworks. The Wagon Wheel Theater is also recognized for bringing wholesome family entertainment to its stage.

Plays and parades were held on the canal and the lake. The lighted craft of the Venetian Nights were spectacular, as were these butterfly boats.

Among other pageants and plays, the history of the Native Americans and their influence on the area was taught by real Indians. Actual teepees were erected and visitors were treated to an authentic demonstration of this important heritage.

Lt. L.D. Merrill, a friend of Homer Rodeheaver, rescued a person in Florida but lost his plane in the process of saving their life. Rodeheaver generously helped Merrill acquire another aircraft, which he then used to advertise Rainbow Records, one of the many music businesses Rodeheaver was instrumental in starting in Winona Lake. Rodeheaver (left) is seen here with Lieutenant Merrill in front of the aircraft.

Posing in front of the airplane are, from left to right, Jack Rodeheaver, Ruth Rodeheaver, Lt. L.D. Merrill, and Jack's mother, Betty. Jack Rodeheaver had begun taking flying lessons from Merrill and planned to operate the airplane solo.

On August 26, 1921, Lieutenant Merrill had his plane in Winona Lake and was giving people rides out over the lake in the afternoon. When hauling passengers, he had disconnected the rear-seat controls in order to prevent a passenger from accidentally engaging them. On this particular day, Merrill was teaching Jack Rodeheaver, Homer Rodeheaver's half-brother, how to fly. Jack was in the front at the main controls, and shortly after becoming airborne and gaining about 3,000 feet in altitude, he began to have difficulty. Merrill could not take over because the back-seat controls had been disengaged and he had forgotten to reconnect them. Merrill then attempted to assist Rodeheaver by unfastening his seatbelt in order to reach around the front seat to regain control. At this point, the airplane turned sharply sideways, causing Merrill to fall to his death. Left alone at the controls, the young Rodeheaver could not manage the craft and crashed the airplane into a cornfield near the fairgrounds, where he perished shortly after impact. Jack Rodeheaver's mother and brother were unfortunate witnesses, watching the entire tragedy from in front of their home on Rainbow Point.

This photograph shows the plane Jack Rodeheaver crashed in a tragic, fatal accident.

In memory of his brother, Homer Rodeheaver purchased a large and lovely stained-glass window with a scene representing the Good Shepherd, which was installed in the Winona Lake Presbyterian Church. Today the church is called the Church of the Good Shepherd.

"Ma" Sunday paid for the land on which to build the Winona Lake Presbyterian Church.

James Heaton (third row, with bow tie) and much of his family participated in the Presbyterian Church Choir. His son, George, is second to his left. His granddaughter, Jane, is in the front row, second from right. Music was always an integral part of the lives of those involved in Winona Lake activities.

Sunday morning church services were well attended by devout believers, but even then, it was difficult to cajole people into those front pews. James Heaton, a regular, is three rows back on the right side, again in a bow tie, with his son and grandsons, at the Winona Lake Presbyterian Church.

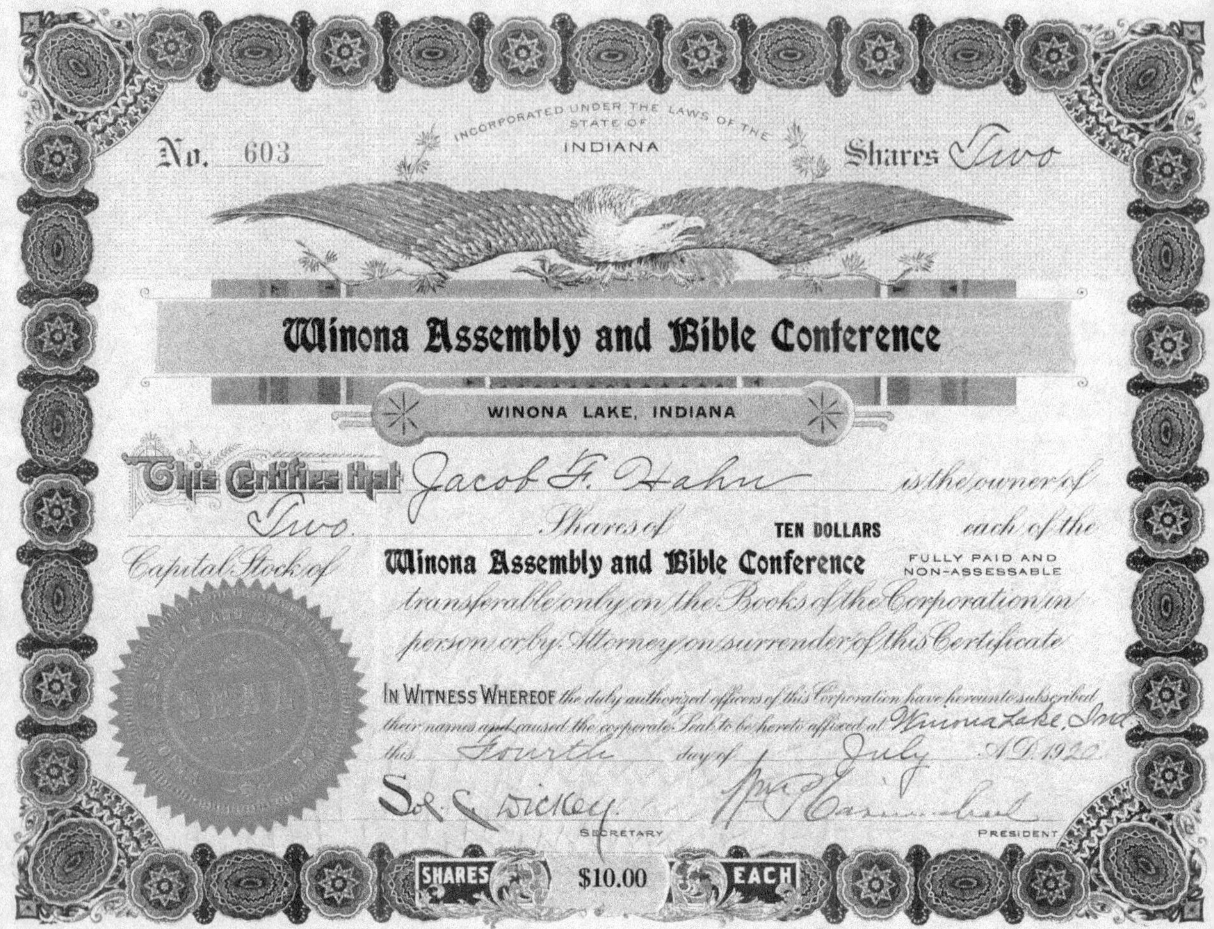

No. 603

INCORPORATED UNDER THE LAWS OF THE STATE OF INDIANA

Shares Two

Winona Assembly and Bible Conference

WINONA LAKE, INDIANA

This Certifies that Jacob F. Hahn is the owner of Two Shares of TEN DOLLARS each of the Capital Stock of **Winona Assembly and Bible Conference** FULLY PAID AND NON-ASSESSABLE transferable only on the Books of the Corporation in person or by Attorney on surrender of this Certificate

IN WITNESS WHEREOF the duly authorized officers of this Corporation have hereunto subscribed their names and caused the corporate Seal to be hereto affixed at Winona Lake, Ind this Fourth day of July A.D. 1920

Sol C. Dickey
SECRETARY

PRESIDENT

SHARES $10.00 EACH

Following the losses from the great fire of 1914, the Winona Assembly suffered a few years of heartbreak followed by financial collapse. The assembly had invested deeply in the interurban railway system, believing there would be a good return on their investment that would provide money for the future. The advent of the automobile turned that dream into a crashing failure that devastated the assembly. In the end, they had no choice but to declare bankruptcy and close many of their doors. It was a shattering time for those who knew what great works had been accomplished by this organization. After much prayer and reorganization, a new entity was created that was able to turn that failure into success. The Winona Assembly and Bible Conference was a nonprofit corporation restricted from having any debt over $10,000 or from paying any dividends. Early in the reorganization, they were able to establish a method to pay off former debt and creditors, caring for those in most dire need first. They reopened their doors and had over 10,000 workers at their first conference. The fact that this was all accomplished during the trying times of World War I was nothing short of amazing. The success was attributed to much prayer and the work of a number of influential and devout people who came to the aid of the organization when it most needed their support and advice. Shares in this new offering were sold for $10 each.

In 1921, Irvin Van Dyke, who had no job prospects, managed to purchase a house on King's Highway in Winona Lake. The 44-year-old was a family man with four children to feed. Once they moved in to the house, they investigated it thoroughly and discovered a milk-bottling factory in the basement. Van Dyke began buying milk from local farmers, bottling what was not usurped by four hungry children, and selling it. The dairy became successful and eventually Van Dyke was able to sell the business to Ralph and Mary Haney, who named it the Winona Dairy.

Mary Haney wanted a logo for their new Winona Dairy business. Knowing the history of the Potawatomi Indians in the area, they felt an image of an Indian head would be appropriate. They searched and found a young woman who they thought most closely resembled one of the lovely tribe members. They took a throw rug and put it across the shoulders of Airy Anne Haymaker, put a feather in her hair, and turned the finished design into a red logo. Princess Winona adorned the Winona Dairy bottle from that point forward. The house holding the dairy was later moved to the Kelly addition and is now the home of Bill and Joan Darr.

The Rodeheavers pose for a formal portrait signed by Daguerre—famous for the daguerreotype—of Chicago. From left to right are Dr. Joe Rodeheaver, Ruth Rodeheaver, Yumbert Rodeheaver, and Homer Rodeheaver.

The Rodeheaver home, Rainbow Point, was shaped like a boat and overlooked Winona Lake. In 1911, Homer Rodeheaver purchased Hall-Mack Publishers in Philadelphia and moved the business to the Westminster Hotel in Winona Lake. Rodeheaver, who was a noted trombonist and traveled around the world with Billy Sunday, was responsible for much of the music in Winona Lake. James Heaton's son, George, recounts a memory from England, when he was serving in World War II. Heaton was part of a group of soldiers who wanted to have a church service and drove to a bombed-out church. As they cleaned up, George found some song hymnals under the debris. As he opened one, the words "Rodeheaver-Hall-Mack, Winona Lake Indiana" brought tears to his eyes, and he knew the impact that Winona Lake's music had around the world.

The Rodeheavers could step outside a second-floor room and gleefully slide down into the lake. Frequent visitor Will Rogers once wrote a story about "Rody's slide" in one of his columns. Shortly after the publicity, Homer Rodeheaver discovered a large group of uninvited guests assembling on his roof to partake in the "slide ride." Fearing for their safety and not knowing the strength or load-bearing capabilities of his roof, Rodeheaver had the slide disassembled and removed.

The dining porch at Rodeheaver's Rainbow Point home was a popular entertaining spot, and the family frequently hosted guests. One evening, they invited Virgil and Blanche Brock for dinner. Brock was given permission to bring along his blind cousin as well. As the glorious fall sunset was dropping over the lake, they all began describing it, careful to include words for the blind cousin. Suddenly, the young man began describing the scene back to them. "How can you do that?" they asked him. "Because of how you are painting it for me with words," he responded. He paused and then added, "I can see it in vivid detail in my mind. In fact, I can see *beyond* the sunset." Those words put a spark of creativity in Virgil Brock's mind and he began writing on a napkin. By the time dessert was served, the first half of the beautiful song "Beyond the Sunset" had been written.

Fred King was responsible for much of the beauty and flowering plants along the walks and pathways. Some of the plants were tropical plants, which King had to dig up and re-plant on an annual basis. King also owned a grocery store that some folks say influenced the naming of King's Highway. Others say it was because of the religious influence in Winona Lake and that it referred to the biblical "King." King's grocery and service station were open on Sundays and the Fort Wayne Sunday paper was sold there. Old-timers say the Winona Lake officials would scurry in to examine the news. If something negative came out about Winona, the town officers would buy up all the papers so people could not read any bad news about their town.

The Winona Assembly supported all kinds of opportunities to benefit children and adults. Bethany Girls Camp was started by Leo Polman. It was located in the park by Cherry Creek.

Bethany Girls Camp had lovely, clean, and comfortable facilities. The experience of going to camp at Winona Lake was beneficial in many ways and girls went home enriched by their time in camp.

Large crowds participated in the summer camps, giving credence to their value in the lives of these young women. The stone bleachers are still in place, welcoming visitors.

Summer Boys Club was another opportunity to reach young children and give them the benefit of a camp teaching the values of good citizenship, kindness, philanthropy, and striving to do the best in life.

Athletic events like swimming and diving, and lots of other fun activities were included in Boys Club programs.

The Rodeheaver Hall-Mack enterprise employed a number of people. Note the Rodeheaver name on the safe at right.

The musical endeavors of the Rodeheaver Hall-Mack Company reached around the world, so a large staff was necessary to keep it functioning. Two gentlemen, Bruce Howe (fourth row, far left) and Phil Laurien (third row, far left), were local men with very positive involvement in the assembly and Winona Lake over the years.

Rev. George Bernard was another noted musical mind of Winona Lake. Seen here with his wife, Hannah, in front of the Westminster Hotel, Bernard wrote the familiar song, "The Old Rugged Cross."

Music poured out of Winona Lake during the years when Homer Rodeheaver and Billy Sunday took command of the pulpit in the tabernacle. Two brothers, A.H. Ackley (left), a preacher and songwriter, and B.D. Ackley, a songwriter, are seen here in front of the Westminster Hotel, owned at that time by Rodeheaver. One Sunday, near Easter time, A.H. Ackley had just finished preaching when he was approached by a young man who challenged him, saying, "I don't believe anything you said!" Ackley was taken aback and asked, "What specifically is it you don't believe?" "Why should I worship a dead Jew?" the young man answered. Ackley was heartbroken that his sermon had not been well received or understood, and tried to convince the young man that this was what Easter was all about and described to him how Christians believed that Christ had risen and was still alive, not dead. Later that afternoon Ackley switched to another form of persuasion and wrote the famous hymn, "He Lives."

This group shares a meal in the same room at Homer Rodeheaver's Rainbow Point that inspired the song, "Beyond the Sunset." Homer Rodeheaver is at the far end, at the head of the table, and to his left are the Brocks. The Ackleys, also famous songwriters, are at Rodeheaver's right. Elmer Funk is near the camera on the far right.

The face of downtown Winona continued to change. The Rodeheaver Music Store is seen here. "Ma" Sunday would sometimes go to the music store looking for Homer Rodeheaver in order to gain his attendance at the afternoon programs. Rodeheaver, a good man, but not always obedient, would hide in a closet, but "Ma" Sunday was not fooled. "Homer, come out here!" she would demand until he acquiesced.

Ben Phillipson donated the first swans to the Lily Pond. After the graceful birds inhabited the pond, it became known as the Swan Pond.

Traveling together to tent revival meetings around the world, this group made the song "The Old Rugged Cross" a favorite of generations. From left to right are Robert Matthews, the pianist; Virginia Asher, who sang the song as a duet with Homer Rodeheaver (center); "Ma" Sunday; and Billy Sunday, the main speaker at the tent and tabernacle meetings. A large stone cross-shaped tombstone in Oakwood Cemetery near Winona Lake is inscribed with the name "Asher." The reverse side of the cross is etched with the words, "This is not the end." Part of this large triangular-shaped memorial includes stone steps leading to a stone-carved music stand inscribed with the words of the song, "The Old Rugged Cross."

As time progressed in Winona Lake, the characteristics of boat traffic changed. This 1929 photograph shows a group having a tour of the lake.

Katherine Carmichael was the organist and accompaniment for Rodeheaver during the Billy Sunday crusades. Carmichael faithfully held this position for over 40 years. The lovely Carmichael lived next door to Rodeheaver and neither of them ever married.

Famous performer Ernestine Schumann-Heink was a favorite at Winona Lake over the years; her performances were almost always sold out.

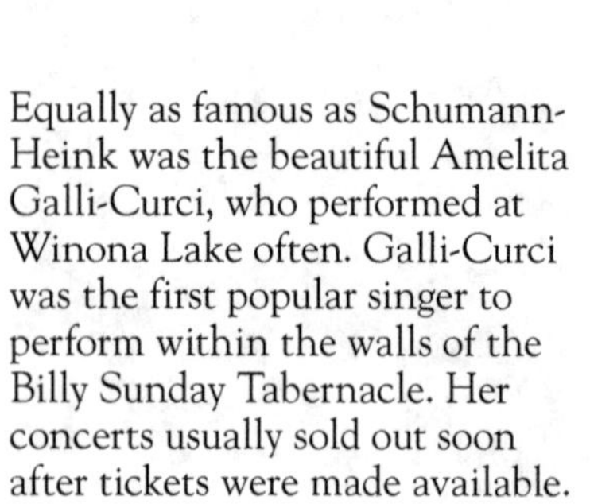

Equally as famous as Schumann-Heink was the beautiful Amelita Galli-Curci, who performed at Winona Lake often. Galli-Curci was the first popular singer to perform within the walls of the Billy Sunday Tabernacle. Her concerts usually sold out soon after tickets were made available.

Jim Heaton, seen here with a "sold out" sign next to the advertisement for the flamboyant Galli-Curci, shows that standing-room-only tickets were all that was available for $1.10.

In August 1928, Will Rogers visited Winona Lake to perform after an invite from Billy Sunday. Blaine Mikesell and George Heaton were both high school students at the time. The boys witnessed the famous Rogers opening, in which the curtains were pulled most of the way back and the crowd was looking at an empty stage. Rogers pulled back one curtain with both hands and peeked out. The audience laughed, and from that point on, Rogers had them in the palm of his hand. During this visit, Rogers met Homer Rodeheaver and heard his amazing slide trombone. Rogers later wrote, "You all know Rody, the great slide trombone player who always led the music in the Billy Sunday Revivals. Rody has slip-horned more sinners into the kingdom of Heaven than any of the old-timers with their trumpets or even the great biblical musician Nero, who never missed a fire and played 'Turkey in the Straw.' He sure can sing. He is the fellow that can make you sing whether you want to or not . . . You know singing does more good than preaching. For when you are singing you haven't got time to think. I want to get back there again next year and see the old gang."

The celebrity violinist Efram Zimbalist, who was born in Russia, had a child and grandchild who became famous actors: Efram Zimbalist Jr., who had a major role in the "F.B.I." drama series; and Stephanie Zimbalist, who costarred in the series "Remington Steele." Efram Zimbalist Sr. performed several times in Winona Lake during these years.

The auditorium and the Tabernacle were not the only places for performances. The Hillside Open-Air Auditorium was often used in afternoons and early evenings for concerts and smaller productions to educate, enlighten, and entertain. The open auditorium received steady use through 1970 and is still used today for church programs, outdoor concerts, and weddings.

The Hillside Open-Air Auditorium drew large crowds, especially when Carmichael took to the stage and Rodeheaver joined in to awe the audience with his skills on the trombone. When the two musicians added their voices and led the crowd, the "hills of Winona" were definitely "alive with the sound of music."

Once the fire of 1914 had subsided, it was recognized that Winona Lake had need of a first-rate fire department. The Winona Lake Fire Department then became "the greatest little fire department on Earth." N. Bruce Howe resides in Winona Lake and became fire chief, with several heroic rescues during his career. In 1956, during a house fire in Winona Lake, two young boys, Jay, 11, and his brother Dale, 14, were in a basement bedroom unconscious. The father had tried unsuccessfully to save his sons. Chief Howe donned an untried piece of equipment—an "air pack"—and went into the inferno. He found both boys and carried them out one at a time. Today Dale Benson is a doctor in Indianapolis, saving lives of his own, and Jay Benson is president of World Missionary Press in New Paris, saving lives in another way.

Four

Transitions
1940–Present

The biblical and evangelistic influences on Winona Lake have been great over the years, but other factors have also shaped the community. Great and generous people have given unselfishly of their time, their wealth, and their talents to create something bigger than themselves.

Beginning with the Beyer brothers, who were intelligent and farsighted businessmen, the community has benefited from their wisdom. They created a great amusement park that attracted thousands to the shores of Winona Lake. They sponsored and assisted those who followed them in, making it not just an entertaining park, but also a place of reflection, learning, education, redemption, worship, and music.

A failure or two did not stop the grand plan of service to others. This signature of service still permeates the atmosphere today. The automobile brought the end of the Interuban Railway, but later it brought many to see an evangelist with, unbelievably, a greater reach than Billy Sunday: Billy Graham. Graham represented the culmination of all that was good about Winona Lake and the assembly.

Transitioning from one kind of outreach to another, a beautiful college came into existence. Old structures came down but improved buildings were erected. New benefactors moved into the area and new companies with great and forward-thinking leadership begin to pick up the slack from the reins of those departing. Brilliant men like Dane Miller and his generous, kind wife, Mary Louise Miller, recognize and share the values that made this community a rich source of inspiration.

A man named Paul Lowman, who lived on Sixth Street, had a pet lion, which he trained to water ski, causing quite a sensation among visitors to Winona Lake. Generally, this performance would take place near the Gakte Building on the northern shore of the lake. In one story that has been repeated over the years, a fellow was changing a flat tire near Sixth Street and the tame lion got away from his owner, meandered over, and laid a gentle paw on the tire changer's shoulder. Thinking a friend had come up to assist him in changing the tire, the fellow turned around and came face to face with a large lion.

Petrie Music School students pose in front of the Winona Hotel during band camp in 1942.

A story from this block in 1928 involved Robinson Grocery, owned by Mabel and Dick Robinson. One summer afternoon, Mrs. Robinson went to the west side of Warsaw to the Groninger family farm to pick up some fresh dairy products for their business. When she returned to Winona and entered her grocery store, she found it unoccupied. Concerned, she located her husband on a back deck overlooking the Winona Canal, with another gentleman. Mrs. Robinson, always a good hostess, asked if either of them would like a fresh glass of buttermilk. The gentleman with her husband said, "I would like that. I don't know how long it has been since I have had a fresh glass of buttermilk." Mrs. Robinson promptly provided her famous, but unexpected guest, Will Rogers, with the cold, fresh treat.

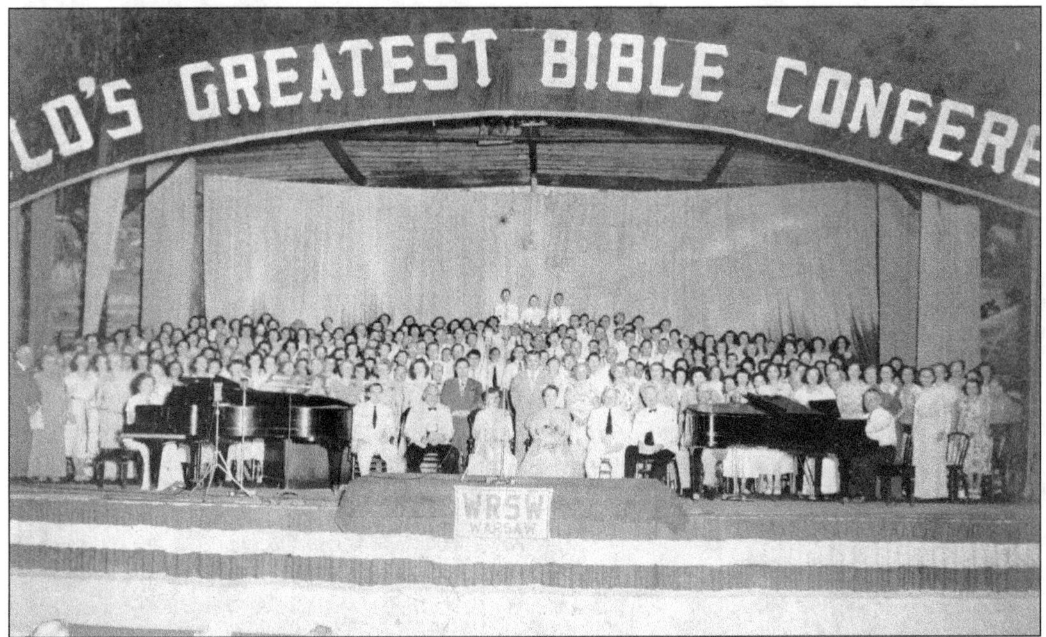

The City of Warsaw grew in parallel with Winona Lake, often intertwining. The close proximity of the two communities has been a benefit to each in many ways. In this case the radio station WRSW of Warsaw was used to spread the word about the "World's Greatest Bible Conference." Twin grand pianos almost don't fit on the large stage of the Tabernacle.

Meade Sheaffer, an understudy of the famous *Saturday Evening Post* artist Norman Rockwell, was a summertime childhood friend of local Phil Laurien. Sheaffer stayed friends over the years and was positively influenced by his time in Winona Lake. Sheaffer and Norman Rockwell used each other as well as their own children as models for the *Saturday Evening Post* cover illustrations. This cover by Sheaffer is titled, "My Childhood Memories of Winona Lake."

The stage was full, but never as full as the seats, at Tabernacle events. Katherine Carmichael is seated at the organ on the left, waiting to play while choir members take a moment to peruse their music. Carmichael kept a photograph album and had a duplicate of this photograph in it marked with an arrow pointing to her own face and a small note that said "me."

The Winona School of Photography, affiliated with the Professional Photographers of America, was in Winona Lake for 80 years. Professional photographers from all over the world came here for summer classes. The school was established in 1900 as the Daguerre Institute, and the Daguerreotype Club gave it to the Professional Photographers of America in 1921. The school was open from mid-May to mid-September, with 1,200 to 1,400 students participating in courses each year. Interestingly, someone on the island once had a hot water heater blow up in the middle of the winter. It took off like a rocket and was not found until the School of Photography re-opened the next spring. It was found inside their building, where fortunately it had not damaged their pride and joy—a theater-type classroom with a rotating stage.

Ed Purrington (first row, far right) was the director of the School of Photography. He had been a chief photographer for the Ford Motor Company for 15 years. Also in the first row, third from left, was Jack Emsile, an instructor, Winona resident, and photographer for the Kodak Company. This distinguished staff kept attendance high at the summer classes.

Rev. Billy Graham had deep roots in Winona Lake, beginning with a job working for "Youth for Christ" on June 13, 1949. Billy Graham, not yet a famous evangelist, was at a meeting in the Rainbow Room of the Westminster Hotel that lasted until 3:00 a.m., contemplating a leadership role. At the end of the meeting, a minister from California said, "Billy Graham will be having an evangelistic tent meeting in a park this fall in California. I believe we should lay hands on Billy." Graham opened his Bible and read Joel 3, which says, "The harvest is ripe, and I'm claiming this for Christ." Witnesses to this meeting later were heard to say, "That meeting room had an amazing atmosphere. It was as if it were electrically charged." When it was time for the tent meeting in the fall, Billy Graham and George Beverly Shea appeared on the popular Stuart Hamblen radio program in Los Angeles. Hamblen was so impressed with the two that he and his wife attended the evening tent meeting and became Christians during it. This made a great impact on Hamblen and he was very vocal about it. A few days later, Hamblen met John Wayne, a friend of his. Wayne said, "What happened to you? It's all over town, something about a church in a tent in a park." Hamblen walked down the street with him, telling him of the experience. That night at midnight, his striking clock woke Hamblen and he found John Wayne was on his mind. The chiming clock struck a musical chord and Hamblen got up to write the song, "It is No Secret." Hamblen's verse, "When the chimes of time ring out the news," was written for John Wayne. Stuart Hamblen became a regular visitor to Winona Lake in the 1950s.

William Randolph Hearst, the newspaper magnate, was also impressed with the young Graham, and gave a lot of publicity to his tent meetings. Graham became well known in a short period of time because of the publicity and the positive reaction he received at the evangelistic meetings. Graham was offered the opportunity to become a full-time evangelist and was promised he would be supported in this ministry should he choose to continue. Graham went back to Winona Lake after these evangelistic efforts and stayed at the Westminster Hotel. He borrowed the keys to the Presbyterian Church next door and had his own all-night prayer meeting, asking God for direction. Would he select Youth for Christ or evangelism? The following morning, Homer Rodeheaver met Graham at the bottom of the stairs in the lobby and asked, "What is your decision?" Graham told him, "I thought I should continue in Youth for Christ, but I think God is calling me to be an evangelist." Rodeheaver responded, "Billy, you had better go the way God is calling you." Reverend Graham became internationally known but always remained loyal to his roots in Winona Lake. This photograph was taken at Rainbow Point years later. Such a friendship had formed that after Homer Rodeheaver died in 1955, Graham requested to stay there and sleep in Rodeheaver's bed. Pictured with Graham are Amrette Leiter, the owner of DePuy Orthopedics; Katherine Carmichael; Helen Sellers; Jim Thomas; Ruth Rodeheaver; and several members of the Graham team.

The times were changing but crowds continued to come to Winona. The crowds no longer had to wave paper fans; there were electric fans to help cool the air. Air conditioning was still a dream for the future, but Billy Graham offered to raise enough money to purchase air conditioning for the Tabernacle. "Ma" Sunday intercepted the offer, saying, "Billy Sunday doesn't need it and it doesn't need it now."

Years after the Tabernacle was erected as a temporary structure, it continued to be utilized and massive crowds continued to come for the blessings they received by attending.

This photograph shows the last time the Tabernacle was used. Heavy rains came that spring and the roof developed many leaks and other safety hazards. The building was no longer comfortable, or safe, inside. It was decided to move to the Rodeheaver Auditorium.

For years, there was a miniature golf course between the hotel and Endicott Chapel.

Automobiles are parked in front of the downtown shops of Winona Lake in the early 1950s.

After the Tabernacle was ruined, further deterioration of facilities occurred. Aged buildings were in disrepair and a decline was happening to the area. Police calls became frequent to an area that had always been free from such activity. The area by the Swiss Terrace became disreputable, and even the Old Glory became tarnished and faded.

Much like their predecessors, Sol Dickey and the Beyer brothers, two people stepped into the breach created by the decline of the area. The president of the Winona Lake Historical Society, the visionary Brent Wilcoxson, wanted to give Winona Lake a new lease on life, so he began approaching many possible donors to obtain capital funding. Dr. Dane and Mary Louise Miller began to look into the possibilities of working with Wilcoxson to organize a rebirth for Winona Lake. Dr. Miller, the founder of the internationally known Biomet Corporation, was able to give some attention to philanthropic efforts to benefit the community.

Wilcoxson wasted little time in obtaining sketches and architectural renderings for the shared vision of a revitalized downtown Winona Lake.

Several residents were invited to meet numerous times in order to exchange ideas and inspiration with the architects. Ideas surfaced such as creating a beautiful panoramic view for drivers to look at as they enter Winona Lake under the viaduct.

An exciting change happened when the Remnant Trust, a national treasure of precious books and documents, was relocated to the replica Billy Sunday Tabernacle in Winona Lake.

The planners for the new village of Winona cleverly utilized existing structures and moved them into place as shops. The buildings were updated and strengthened to create a feeling of going back in time to the days when Winona Lake was at its peak. Each shop was unique and the mix of architecture matched the uniqueness that has always been part of Winona Lake.

Louis Zamperini, the subject of Laura Hillenbrand's book, *Unbroken*, converted at the same Billy Graham tent meeting in California as Stuart Hamblen. Zamperini returned to visit the new village of Winona in the fall of 2011. He met with Dr. Manahan of Grace College and reminded him of his experience with Billy Graham, starting with the all-night prayer meeting in the Rainbow Room in the Westminster Hotel. Zamperini was horribly mistreated and tortured by his Japanese captors during World War II. *Unbroken* is about Zamperini and his decision to forgive those who had harmed him so severely. Zamperini gave credit to all who continue to provide purpose and inspiration to people, such as Billy Graham, and to those who support ministries such as the one that saved him from a life of bitterness. Winona Lake remained in his mind for being that kind of place.

The new Winona 1000 Park Bake Café is in the updated old music building.

The old boat house was an acknowledged landmark for years, so it was very appropriate to use the building as a lovely restaurant, shop, and offices. The Boat House Restaurant stands with pride over the old foundation and has the same dazzling view of the sunset.

Another town landmark, this sculpture, *The Student*, still invites guests to the Swan Pond. A small island was created for this work of art from Paris. Visitors can still come to admire, or, in the case of art students from Grace College, sit and sketch the beautiful scene. Just a stone's throw away is the Garfield, the home of Dr. Ken Taylor, the author of *The Living Bible* and founder of Tyndale Press, who moved his family here when he was teaching at Wheaton College in Illinois. During his long commute, he worked on his favorite project. Taylor felt that the Bible needed to be paraphrased so children and adults could read it easily. The now-famous *Living Bible* is yet another example of Winona Lake's far-reaching and lasting impact on society.

The lovely old Westminster Hotel also went through a rebirth. It now houses the Reneker Museum, which is full of nostalgic and historical items about Winona Lake. Also in the hotel are the fortunate students from Grace College who now use rooms from the refurbished hotel as their dorms. Many of these students do not realize the tremendous musical history associated with their dorm. In 1913, C. Austin Miles, a frequent visitor, photographer, and songwriter, was asked to write a song about hope for a new hymnal, using the Bible verses in John 20 involving Mary Magdalene. Miles, as a photographer, envisioned seeing a lady early in the morning going to the tomb. He wrote as if he could see the event take place through the eyes of his camera, and the familiar song "In the Garden" was born.

The canal was in disrepair, so new seawalls were erected and debris was removed and dredged out. This is a view of Winona Village during one of the annual highlights of the year, the June Art Fair and Exhibition. Artists from all over join permanent resident artists, and their shops, to display art. Tents pop up like mushrooms for all the activity. A competition is held with a generous prize to the various winners. The event is popular and well attended.

During the Art Fair, visitors are treated to music and food booths in various locations on the grounds. The musical heritage continues with Jazz combos, chamber music, and antique instrumental groups all providing entertainment.

Although Winona Lake now has a home numbering system, old named homes such as this one—the Baldwin—maintain their identity. Many of the homes in the area have been part of a historical renovation project and are refurbished beautifully. Tours are offered on a regular basis by cooperating owners. This lovely home has been restored by Brad and Deb Bishop.

The canal has been an integral part of the Winona Lake story since it was first built. Today, it is a lovely home for a variety of boats, boaters, and their nearby residences. In the old days, the milkman delivered milk on a route all around Winona Lake along the canal, including the Billy Sunday home. Fred Cromer, the son of the Presbyterian minister, delivered milk early in the morning to the Sunday family. Once when he delivered it, Reverend Sunday made quite a spectacle of himself as he urgently ran to catch Cromer with a change in their order. "Fred, Fred!" he called, "We want two quarts of milk today!" Cromer turned in time to see that Reverend Sunday was wearing only a shirt, a necktie, a vest, and garters for his socks—but no trousers.

They started it all. The Beyer Home is a beautifully restored Indiana limestone structure. The home now sits proudly overlooking what was once a wilderness. The heritage left by this family continues to influence all who visit.

The area continues to be revitalized and is now an important center for orthopedics. Associated businesses have joined with Grace College to build a lovely new auditorium on the campus, where Winona Lake can once again provide a venue for guest speakers and enriching educational programs, such as the recent visit and heartwarming speech by former first lady Laura Bush.

A lovely place to live, the village of Winona and Winona Lake also offer much to visitors. In honor of its many influential predecessors, there are plans to make the area a place of refuge, inspiration, family entertainment, education, and more, for the foreseeable future.

www.ingramcontent.com/pod-product-compliance
Lightning Source LLC
LaVergne TN
LVHW081559100826
845153LV00004B/420
9781531663940